ANTIQUE & CLASSIC
AIRCRAFT

ANTIQUE & CLASSIC

David Davies
& Mike Vines

AIRCRAFT

CHANCELLOR
PRESS

First published in 1985 by Osprey Publishing
Reprinted 1989

This edition published in 1997 by Chancellor Press,
an imprint of Reed International Books Limited
Michelin House, 81 Fulham Road, London SW3 6RB

British Library Cataloguing in Publication Data

Davies, David
    Antique & classic airplanes
    – (Osprey colour series)
    I. Airplanes – History
    I. Title II. Vines, Mike
    629.133'340422 TL685.1
ISBN 1 85152 815 6

Printed in Hong Kong

A Cessna twin flew over a boring photography class at the College of Art and Design in Birmingham, England, in 1964 and two pairs of eyes followed it—Air Portraits was born. From that moment partners David Davies and Mike Vines knew they were hooked on airplanes.

Mike (pictured on the right) started photographing airplanes at the age of 14 after being introduced to aircraft recognition by an uncle in the Observer Corps. He survived seven years as a photographer/air observer for the British Ministry of Defence and now, aged 42, runs the photo studio for a large international company.

David's interest began even earlier, when at the tender age of 13 he was guest of honour at the last Battle of Britain air display at the famous wartime airfield of Castle Bromwich in Warwickshire. Now aged 41, he divides his time between his normal job as a local government photographer with as much aviation photography as he can squeeze in.

Air Portraits have been the official photographers to the Shuttleworth Collection for 15 years and are contributing photographers to the British general aviation magazine *Pilot*.

Based in the West Midlands, their speciality is air-to-air photography. This can be a frustrating pastime in Britain, for not only do the usual problems of aircraft availability exist, but the totally unreliable British weather also has to be taken into account.

Between them they have flown in over a 100 different types of aircraft. In 1970 David gained his private pilots license and for a short time held a share in a Stampe. They always *insist* on a full and proper briefing before starting air-to-air photography. The necessity of this procedure was brought home to them back in the early seventies with the Rothmans team. David takes up the story . . .

'We were out to get the inverted Stampe shot on page 123. Iain Weston was to oblige with the inverted machine and the late Neil Williams was to fly me in the Stampe cameraship. We briefed and made for the planes. I was strapped into the front cockpit, kneeling on the seat looking backwards with the harness over the back of my legs. In my hands I had my new camera, about to take its first air-to-air pictures. The evening was beautiful and the planned shots were soon in the can. As we cruised back to the aerodrome in tight formation for landing I thought it would be a good idea to shoot some knife-edge shots of Iain's Stampe. As I had no radio contact with my pilot, I gestured to Neil with one of my hands what I wanted. I thought he would pass this message on to Iain who would pull up into a knife-edge for the camera, but instead I saw the horizon begin to rotate around *our* tailplane as we began to roll around the other Stampe. My first reaction was to grab the cockpit sides, as I felt a little insecure kneeling there, but I would have to release my new camera! The other Stampe flashed by underneath of us and I was not at all concerned that I had missed the shot. Fortunately Neil knew what he was doing and kept positive G on all the way round and before I could make a decision on what to do we were right way up again. It was comforting to know that I was flying with the man who was thirteen times British Aerobatic Champion.'

Unlike the majority of photographers in this field they do not normally use 35 mm film. Both trained as industrial and commercial photographers and use large format cameras (up to 10″ × 8″). For aviation work they initially used Pentacon Six outfits, producing 2¼″ square negatives on 120 roll film. After about twelve years service these were replaced by Pentax 6 × 7 cm cameras which also use 120 roll film. As the name suggests, these produce negatives of 6 × 7 cm (2¼″ × 2¾″).

Nearly all the illustrations in this book were exposed on Kodak Ektachrome roll film, although recently they have been trying the new Fuji materials.

For the purposes of this book, 'Antique' is defined as a light airplane built before 1946, while 'Classic' is used to describe airplanes built between 1946 and 1955.

Antique & Classic Airplanes is a full colour spectacular devoted to what many purists consider to be real airplanes: Stearmans, Tiger Moths, Monocoupes, and many more. Most of the airplanes featured are still active, kept in airworthy condition by tender loving care and often flown by pilots to relive the age of leather flying helmets, silk scarves, and the quest for adventure.

This book captures the art and technology of private flying over five decades, from the twilight of the Edwardian era, through the roaring twenties, dapper thirties, and the stylish modernity of the forties and fifties. *Antique & Classic Airplanes* features close-up detail and concentrates on evocative air-to-air photography.

Front cover Ryan PT-22 Recruit. **Title pages** de Havilland Dragon Rapide. **Back cover** Detail of Arrow Active II

Bernt Bjorkman's Auster 6a Tugmaster is based at Vasteros, Sweden. Pictured at the PFA Rally at Cranfield in 1983, SE-ELG was previously VF600 with the British Army as an AOP.6 artillery spotter and light communications aircraft. It still has auxiliary aerofoil flaps extending aft of the wing trailing edge to improve short field performance and a high-visibility cabin door. The aptly named Tugmaster was used as a glider tug and powered by a 145 hp D.H. Gipsy Major 10 Mk 1-1 engine

Contents

Stick and string

Three of the world's earliest flying machines sit timelessly on the grass at Old Warden airfield, near Bedford, England, awaiting the calm conditions required to allow them to take to the air, just as they did 75 years ago. The 1910 French Deperdussin (nearest), 1910 British Avro Triplane IV, and a 1909 French Bleriot Type XI all use wing-warping for roll control

9

Left The Y-shaped 35 hp Anzani engine allowed the Deperdussin to achieve sustained cross-country flights. **Above** The basic rigging of the Deperdussin: king posts above and below keep the wing rigid enough to give the wing-warping wires enough movement for positive control

Overleaf When the weather is kind the Deperdussin is walked to the end of the runway and its tiny engine swung into life. Despite its age the 'Dep' can still complete a circuit of the airfield. **Inset** Jules Verne-style cockpit features a huge control wheel aft of the four gallon brass fuel tank

A wooden jig keeps the Blackburn Monoplane's triangular fuselage square during maintenance. The wooden safety bar across the pilot's seat is augmented by a modern harness. Aviators of old didn't seem to miss the electronic gismos we take for granted today: the instrument panel is dominated by the rev counter, and a large brass Victorian magneto switch is located to the left of the control wheel. Three throttle levers are used to keep the rotary engine twirling, its beat punctuated by a 'blip' switch to reduce airspeed for landing. **Right** The half-cowled engine of the 1912 Blackburn is a 7-cylinder Gnome rotary of 50 hp

Far left The ignition cut-out or 'blip' button on the Blackburn's large control wheel can impart powerful electric shocks to forgetful pilots who leave their gloves behind. The wheel operates in a strange manner: up and down for elevator control, and turned conventionally to activate the many cables and pulleys which assist the wing-warping. **Above** Wires attached to a pylon above the fuselage absorb the landing shocks while those fixed to the undercarriage take the stress of flying. The Blackburn has a conventional rudder and tailplane which is also wire braced. **Left** A short wooden ladder is required to mount the Blackburn in a gentlemanly manner. **Overleaf** Used at the Blackburn Flying School at Hendon in 1912, the Blackburn is the oldest original British airplane still flying anywhere in the world

Left Replica Avro Triplane IV was built for the motion picture *Those Magnificent Men in their Flying Machines* by the Hampshire Aeroplane Club at Southampton. Rather than succumb to the temptation to build-in modern ailerons, the builders used wing-warping on the two upper sets of wings, and significantly the Triplane was regarded as the best flying machine during the making of the film. A 1927 Cirrus Hermes of 105 hp allows displays to be flown in favourable conditions

This genuine Bleriot Type XI was one of the original airplanes used for instruction at the Bleriot School at Hendon in 1910. The 25 hp Anzani engine has three cylinders in fan-form, almost hidden behind the handsome hand-carved wooden propeller

Below When the wind subsides on cool summer evenings the Bleriot is made ready for flight. Equipped with the mandatory reversed cap and goggles, British Aerospace test pilot John Lewis is loving every minute of it. He is normally employed on the VC10 tanker programme. **Right** Desmond Penrose working hard to get both wheels back on the ground. **Opposite page** The late Neil Williams takes the Bleriot to over 30 feet during a straight hop. The comment which greeted Neil on landing after he had barely cleared the fence at the end of the runway was 'Ah monsieur Bleriot, this week the fence—next week the Channel!'

Opposite page From some angles the Boxkite looks more like a garden fence than an aeroplane. An exposed Desmond Penrose grips the long control stick and prepares to defy gravity. The fuel tank behind him feeds a 90 hp Lycoming. **Above** A refined version of Henry Farman's design, the Boxkite was originally built by the Bristol Aeroplane Company Ltd, and was the first British airplane to be exported; eight examples were ordered by the Imperial Russian Army. **Left** A rare cross-country outing. **Overleaf** Even with a Lycoming engine the Boxkite is a challenge to fly and requires a strong arm to tame it. Full throttle speed is only 30 mph.

Hand swinging a propeller as large as the Avro 504s is hard labour—hence the Hucks Starter. Based a Model-T Ford chassis, the long shaft rotates the propeller hub and is driven via chains and sprockets. When the engine fires the shaft automatically disengages. **Right** Avro 504K over a Bedfordshire backdrop. **Overleaf** Don Cashmore's stunning Sopwith Tabloid replica

28

de Havilland: Moths, Dragons, and Chipmunks

Left One of the most successful light airplanes of all time, this particular de Havilland Moth (G-EBWD) was purchased in 1932 by Richard Shuttleworth and has spent over 50 years at Old Warden. **Above** '*Miss Kenya* to the holding point please.' Angus McVitie, chief test pilot of the College of Aeronautics at Cranfield, willingly obliges. **Overleaf** Everyone, including pilot McVitie (second left), has to help to pull out this big biplane. This D.H.51 is the sole survivor of three examples built between 1924–25.

Designed to carry two or three people, depending on luggage, the type proved too big and too expensive and was not a commercial success. *Miss Kenya*, G-EBIR/VP-KAA, was the first aircraft registered in Kenya and was active there for nearly 40 years before being shipped back to the UK in 1972 for preservation at Old Warden. It is powered by a 120 hp Airdisco 8-cylinder upright Vee engine developed from a 80 hp Renault

A gentle giant, *Miss Kenya* has a beautiful four-blade propeller. **Right** Agility is not a strongpoint of the D.H.51, described as 'unbelievably docile' by its pilots, but it can be flown with élan when the need arises

Completed in time for the 1923 Light Aeroplane Trials at Lympe, this lightweight performed loops and rolls for the crowd—a most impressive performance on a 750 cc Douglas motorcycle engine. Despite being tiresome and unreliable the engine allowed the Humming Bird to cover 59.3 miles on a single gallon of fuel. This example, the first prototype, is powered by an ABC Scorpion twin of 34 hp

Left and above D.H.60X Hermes Moth G-EBWD was the personal fly-about of Richard Shuttleworth who bought it at Brooklands in 1932. A successful racing driver, he used this Moth to travel between his country home at Old Warden and circuits such as Brooklands, where he also kept his original workshop. Soon after acquiring 'WD, he re-engined it with the 105 hp Hermes II 4-cylinder upright in-line which remains in the aeroplane today, over half a century later. **Overleaf, both pages** A 'Moth Meet' over Old Warden airfield: G-ATBL, a Gipsy Moth, is being flown by Tony Haig-Thomas and has a photographer at work in the front seat; G-EBWD is Shuttleworth's own Hermes Moth; and G-EBLV is a Cirrus Moth owned by British Aerospace, the current name for the company which swallowed up de Havilland via the British Aircraft Corporation and Hawker Siddeley Aviation. During this sortie a Pentacon 6 screw-on lens hood disappeared from the photo-ship G-EBWD, never to be seen again

A walk-around look at D.H.6oG Gipsy Moth A-ABAG: **Left** A gleaming copper fuel pipe leads down from the gravity tank located in the centre section of the upper wing. The long exhaust pipe doubles as a hand warmer—sheer bliss for pilot and passenger alike in chilly conditions. **Right** The rear cockpit is a model of simplicity. Big, easy to read instruments encourage the pilot to concentrate on flying the airplane. **Below** Careful detailing was important to de Havilland. **Bottom right** External control cables lead to the rudder and elevators. **Overleaf** Equally happy 'in Spitfires and on motorcycles,' test pilot John Lewis loafs around the circuit at Old Warden before G-ABAG was repainted

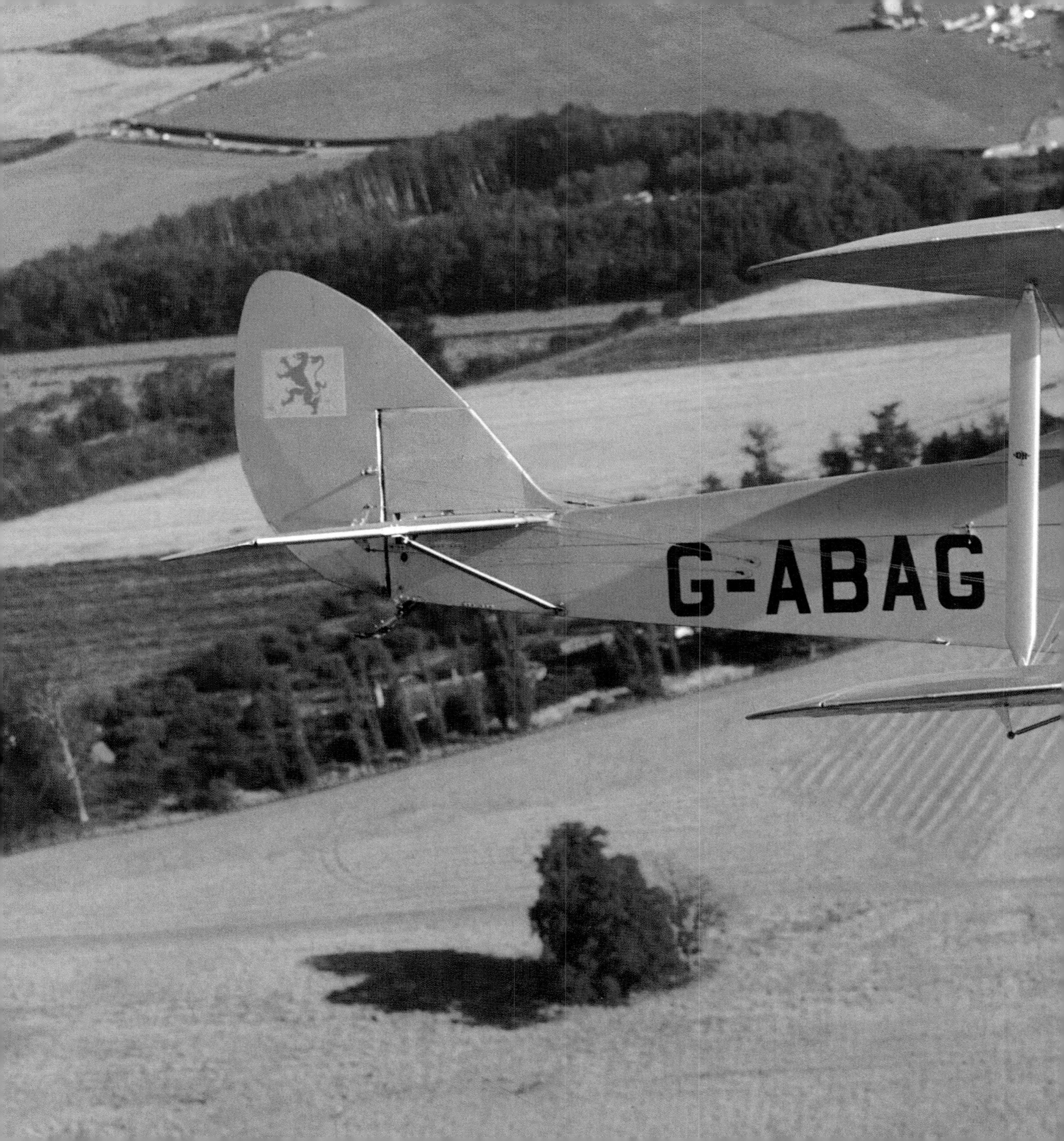
G-ABAG

G-AAVJ, a D.H.6oM Gipsy Moth, was originally built under license by the Moth Aircraft Corporation in the United States. Restorer Ron Souch completed this impeccable rebuild at Hamble in 1985. **Below** Owner Robin Livett (rear cockpit) and Mike Vaisey (proud owner of a D.H.6oG), wait for a 'green' before departing Old Warden for the Moth's home base at Sywell near Northampton

Left Exquisite logo of the Moth Aircraft Corporation. **Below** A brass-mounted compass and neatly welded exhaust pipe compliment this D.H.60M Gipsy Moth. 'Spinning Prohibited' placard on the instrument panel is deadly serious—pilots foolish enough to *literally* take her for a spin had better come equipped with a parachute. **Right** Two thousand feet under your wings, 60 mph on the wind-operated pressure plate ASI, and a clear sky. Who could ask for more! (D.H.60X Hermes Moth, G-EBWD)

The late Air Commodore Alan Wheeler flying his immaculate D.H.82A Tiger Moth when it was adorned in period Brooklands Aviation colours. First flown in 1931, over 7000 Tiger Moths were manufactured before and during WW 2 as basic trainers. Demobilization produced a glut of cheap Tiger's and they were disposed of by the Air Ministry for a flyaway cost of £100 apiece. The 130 hp Gipsy Major powerplant is renowned for its oil spraying qualities

The Tiger Moth is often used for crazy flying displays. G-ACDC, owned by the Tiger Club, bounds aloft. **Overleaf** The oldest active Tiger Moth, 'ACDC is the pride of the Tiger Club fleet. Formed in 1956 and founded by Norman Jones, the Club plays a vital role in keeping the old biplane airworthy. This example was delivered new to the de Havilland School of Flying in 1933

Preceding page Shuttleworth's Tiger Moth (inset) wears the RAF trainer Scheme A uniform originally adopted in 1941. Masquerading as a military machine, civil Tiger G-ANKK is finished in overall yellow, a colour common to RAF trainers in the 1930s. Sywell's hangars are in the background. **This page** For many years Britain's only registered seaplane—a curious paradox for one of the world's foremost maritime nations—Tiger Moth G-AIVW was operated by the Tiger Club and dubbed 'Sea Tiger'. It made its first flight as a floatplane in July 1963. **Right** Keith Sissons, currently accustomed to the controls of a HeavyLift Airlines' Shorts Belfast, puts on a lively display despite the weight and drag of the enormous Edo floats once fitted to an Aeronca Sedan

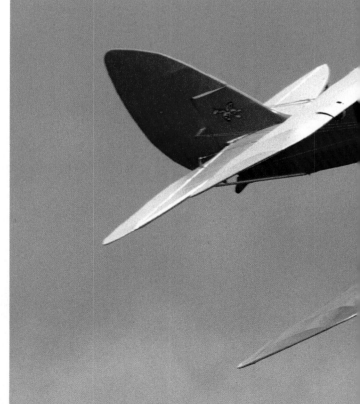

Left A D.H.85 Leopard Moth looks on as D.H.83 Fox Moth G-ACEJ taxies out. The Fox Moth retained the landing gear, engine mounting, wings and tail unit of the Tiger Moth, but it could carry up to four passengers on roughly the same power. **Above and below** The pilot stayed out in the cold, well back in the fuselage. **Overleaf** 'Echo Juliet' is affectionately remembered for her joy riding exploits at Southport Sands. Hugh Field, formerly general aviation editor of *Flight International* magazine, and now public relations manager for the BAe 146 airliner, takes the old Fox up for an airing after a recent respray. Built in 1933, 'EJ was destroyed by fire at Old Warden in 1982

Preceding page Brian Skillicorn is flying this 1934 D.H.85 Leopard Moth. The 130 hp Gipsy Major was capable of delivering a maximum speed of 137 mph, but a cruising speed of around 100 mph is probably a more realistic figure today. Two passengers can be accommodated on the bench seat behind the pilot.
This page Although the type was not a genuine commercial success, 165 Hornet Moths were built. The side-by-side, two-seat enclosed cabin was regarded as a timely step forward from the open cockpit Gipsy Moth. This red machine is a D.H.87B, identified by its squared-off wing tips. Unusually, the landing gear fairings can be turned through ninety degrees to act as airbrakes

Left Part-owner Martin Barraclough completes his
pre-flight before displaying the Dragonfly. This
D.H.90 Dragonfly was shipped from South Africa in
a crate and returned to the UK for restoration to full
airworthiness. Sold at the 1983 Christie's aircraft
auction to Charles Osborn of Louisville, Kentucky,
for £36,000, it stepped over the pond after an epic
45-day ferry flight (which must be a book in itself);
the Dragonfly never missed a beat, but the Atlantic
weather made few concessions to age or beauty. Based
at Clark County Airport, Indiana as N90DH (what
else?), the Dragonfly is flown to air shows across the
nation by Osborn and Larry Lindsey and has scooped
six Grand Champion Trophies. Formerly CR-AAB
and ZS-CTR (and pictured here as G-AEDU), the
Dragonfly is powered by two 130 hp Gipsy Majors,
has a maximum speed of 144 mph, a cruise of 125
mph, and a range of 625 miles

Preceding page A D.H.89A Dragon Rapide (read Dominie in military service) and a Dragonfly give a convincing impersonation of the Short-Mayo composite flying boat/seaplane combination. **Left** A workhorse for over thirty years in airlines big and small, the Dragon Rapide performed reliably worldwide. Notwithstanding its quaint epithet, speed is not a quality that springs to mind when one thinks about this 'gentleman's aerial carriage', but a New Zealand-registered Rapide entered the MacRobertson Trophy Race to Australia and came fifth. **Below** A low-wing successor to the Moth biplane, the D.H.94 Moth Minor was produced in open cockpit or 'coupé' form from 1937. A 90 hp Gipsy Minor gave this model a cruising speed of 100 mph. By September 1939 over 100 Moth Minors had been built at Hatfield, but because of the war effort production was transferred to de Havilland Aircraft Pty at Banksdown, Australia

Grosvenor House, the only survivor of five D.H.88 Comet racers, was a mess under its immaculate shiny red paint when this picture was taken. G-ACSS has not flown since 1939 and languished in a gradually deteriorating condition until serious restoration work began in 1973. Most of the original airframe and innards were rotten and the Comet has been virtually re-manufactured over the past decade.

It won the England to Australia air race (Mildenhall–Melborne) in 1934 ahead of a Douglas DC-2 in just 70 hours 54 minutes. Named after the famous Grosvenor House Hotel, the aircraft was ordered by the hotel's managing director and flown to victory by C. W. A. Scott and Tom Campbell-Black. Three Comets were built specially for the race (in nine months flat) and they featured a wing with a thin aerofoil section, hand-cranked retractable landing gear, and variable pitch propellers. Capable of 220 mph, the Comet had a range of approximately 2925 miles—the first stop during the race to Australia was Baghdad. *Grosvenor House* will almost certainly fly again in 1986, and the limitless patience of the restoration team will be rewarded by the sight of its slippery shape cutting through the air once more

Overleaf Introduced into RAF service in 1950, the Chipmunk was the first aircraft design produced by de Havilland Canada, and it replaced the Tiger Moth in the *ab initio* training role. A small number are still operated by the RAF's Flying Selection Squadron at Swinderby. These Chipmunks, painted in standard RAF training colours, were still in the air force inventory at Church Fenton, Yorkshire, in 1974

75

Left Bob Mitchell looks up through the clear canopy of his DHC-1 Chipmunk Mk 22A, one of a number of civil examples to get the Bristol Aeroplane Company treatment. Apart from the extra Perspex, other modifications included wheel spats, an anti-collision beacon, and wing luggage lockers. **This page** The 'Chippy' was superseded by the Bulldog (many instructors thought the new trainer a step backwards), and ex-RAF machines were expected to be snapped-up on the civil market. Unfortunately the authorities insisted on a number of pointless, expensive modifications, and ownership of this crisp handling classic is still a dream for most private pilots

Americana

1023 Ryan PT-22 Recruit primary trainers were built for the US Services and operated by civilian flying schools to produce the Army and Navy pilots of yesteryear. Bob Mitchell's 'new Recruit' came from Hurley Boehler of Tulsa and it is currently based at Coventry in the British Midlands. Loops, stall turns and snap rolls are included in Mitchell's air show routine, a tribute to the Ryan's flying qualities and sturdy construction. The 160 hp Kinner radial is standard equipment, but the flowing white scarf is an optional extra

Cliff Lovell's magnificent Model 90A Monocoupe (N19432) is powered by a 90 hp Lambert R266 radial. **Below** A big, beautiful biplane, the Boeing Stearman was built for the US Army and Navy and moulded many a young tyro into a skilled pilot. This authentically painted US Navy Stearman is owned by Lindsay Walton. **Right** A Stearman adorned in a sunburst colour scheme

The Honourable Patrick Lindsay is the current owner of this Great Lakes 2T-1A, powered by a Warner R500 Super Scarab 165 with an inverted fuel and oil system to maximize its aerobatic potential. **Right and inset** Built by the Aeronautical Corporation of America Incorporated, better known as Aeronca, G-AEFT was one of a batch of 16 C-3s assembled in Britain during the early 1930s. The airplane accommodates two people side-by-side and its 2-cylinder Aeronca E113 engine gives a cruising speed of 87 mph. When this picture was taken, 'FT was owned by Lieutenant C. E. Humphreys, RN, and based at Royal Naval Air Station Yeovilton, hence the White Ensign on the rudder

Left This Pitts S-1S Special was Gene Soucy's mount at the 1970 World Aerobatic Championships. Curtis Pitts designed this quintessential aerobatic biplane in 1944 and after being up-dated with redesigned aerofoils and a series of more powerful Lycoming engines (currently 260 hp), the little Pitts achieved immortality on the world aerobatic stage after TWA-pilot Bob Herendeen showed the way by coming third in the 1968 Championships. Frank Christensen (of Christen Eagle fame) now owns the production rights. The current two-seat S-2B costs around $75,000 and

it's a real rocket ship. Maximum rate of climb is 2800 feet per minute and the rate of roll is a mind numbing 240 degrees per second. **Above** Mary Gaffaney is the US Ladies National Aerobatic Champion and this her S-1S. **Overleaf** Between 1945–49, Cessna built 2171 of these two-seat Model 120s. Powered by an 85 hp Continental C-85-12 flat-four, the 120 has a respectable 120 mph top speed. G-JOLY is pictured at the PFA Rally at Cranfield in 1984

R. E. Kenneth and Royce Rearwin formed Rearwin Aeroplanes Incorporated in 1929. They developed the 8135T Cloudster (top left) from the standard model in response to a Pan American Airways requirement for an instrument trainer. G-BGAV retains the two separate compartments equipped with a full set of blind-flying instruments. It is powered by a Ken Royce 7G radial. **Above** Bob Willies' Cessna 195 Businessliner is the only one of its type in Europe. The turbocharged 350 hp Jacobs usually has power to spare. **Left** Bowker Air Services use this Aeronca 7AC Champion as a hack to support their crop spraying operations. Over 10,000 Champions were built between 1946–51 and they remain popular because of the economy conferred by a 65 hp Lycoming and their rugged construction. **Overleaf** Currently based at Bad Ragaz in Switzerland and owned by Swissair captain John Greenland, this Fairchild 24 UC-61K made its first flight at Hagerstown, Maryland, in May 1944 and was allocated the USAAF serial 43-14988. It was subsequently operated by the RAF as HB714. Powered by a 200 hp Ranger (the majority had a Warner Scarab), HB-EPF differs from a standard UC-61K by having an additional support strut for each undercarriage leg and a set of wheel spats

British eccentricity

The Granger brothers were responsible for the one-off Archaeopteryx sweptwing semi-tailless ultralight which first flew in October 1930. It has a conventional fin and rudder but wing tip elevons are used for pitch/roll control; they operate symmetrically as elevators and differentially as ailerons—what could be simpler? **Overleaf** 'Thumbs-up' and the 35 hp Bristol Cherub chugs into life. The tiny cockpit is cramped to say the least so the throttle is mounted externally, tacked-on to the side of the fuselage. **Overleaf, top right** Power is not abundant and the pilot must remember to retract his elbows if any climb performance is required. He is entertained by a series of pitch oscillations during take-off and landing, but when the ground is left behind Archaeopteryx is easier to fly than pronounce

Below The late Manx Kelly slides his Chilton DW.1A towards the open door of a Cessna 172. Originally fitted with a French-built 44 hp Train 4T engine, this machine reached 126 mph to win the Folkstone Trophy Race in 1939. **Overleaf** Parnall Elf G-AAIN pictured over Richard Shuttleworth's country seat (now an agricultural college). This Elf is the sole survivor of three examples built between 1928 and 1932. It is powered by a 105 hp Hermes II 4-cylinder upright in-line engine, giving a cruise of 103 mph and a range of 400 miles

The world's only airworthy Spartan Arrow (G-ABWP) over the aqueous environs of Sywell airfield. A total of 28 examples were built by the Spartan Aircraft Company between 1930–32. **Top right** Airline captain John Pothecary in his smart 1932 Redwing II trainer. A mere twelve Redwings were built and this is the only surviving example. It is powered by an Armstrong-Siddeley Genet IIA 5-cylinder radial rated at 80 hp and its red wings fold back for storage. **Right** Not wot it seems, this Super Wot homebuilt is painted in cloned pre-war US Navy markings

Left and above Immaculate in its sparkling aluminium coat, Blackburn B.2 G-AEBJ is maintained in flying trim by British Aerospace. This side-by-side trainer (rather radical in 1932) was only used in small numbers. **Right** The late Bill Woodhams at the controls of his Comper Swift G-ACFT, better known as the *Scarlet Angel*. Once upon a time it belonged to a tea planter in Assam, India. **Overleaf** The one and only Arrow Active II ever built looks superb as it bathes in December sunshine

Opposite page Desmond Penrose was waiting for two name plates to complete the cockpit of his Arrow Active when this picture was taken. The brass screws are already in position on the right. The Active won the 1932 King's Cup air race and Penrose has spent two years restoring it to *concours* condition. **Left** Based on the popular German Klemm L25, this Swallow II was constructed by the British Aircraft Manufacturing Company Ltd in 1937. The substantial two-blade prop is turned by a Pobjoy radial through a gearbox which makes a sound all of its own. **Above** Hugh Field swoops the Swallow over Old Warden. It is reported that one was coaxed to soar, engine off, over Dunstable Downs for 20 minutes

Classic lines: Miles and Percival

This page and overleaf, top left Three Miles Hawk Speed Sixes were made and G-ADGP, an M.2L, is the only one left. Ron Paine raced this ship against a Mew Gull in the National Air Races from 1949, and it held the 100 km closed-circuit speed record in Class C.16 at 192.83 mph. More recently, after a complete rebuild in 1971, it came second in the King's Cup the following year

The Miles M.17 Monarch was the last civil airplane produced by the company before WW 2; 11 were built between 1938–39. G-AFLW was used as a hack by Rolls-Royce Ltd until 1958 and has passed through the hands of several private owners since. Piloted by Dr Ian Dalziel, it took second place in the 1985 Digital Schneider Trophy race. The Monarch can carry two passengers at a cruising speed of 130 mph for up to 600 miles. It is powered by a 130 hp Gipsy Major 1

Left Percy Blamire taxies in after a recent King's Cup air race in his Miles M.65 Gemini 3c G-ALZG, with the racing number 80 underwing. The Gemini was one of the most successful post-war British twins—production began in 1946 and around 130 were built within a year. **Below** G-AKKB was registered on 26 February 1948 and it is currently based at Staverton Airport near Gloucester

Edward Eves' Miles M.3A Falcon was built in 1936 and was registered in Sweden until it returned to Britain in 1963. G-AEEG was restored by Doug Bianchi of Personal Plane Services. **Overleaf** The famous mount of Alex Henshaw, Percival Mew Gull G-AEXF recorded an average speed of 235.25 mph to win the 1938 King's Cup and they made a sensational record flight to the Cape in 1939. It was restored by two members of the Tiger Club, Tom Storey and Martin Barraclough, and the quality of their work is advertised by Boeing 737 captain Brian Smith as he emphasizes the Mew Gull's penetrating shape. Sadly, the airplane hit a ditch when it landed at Redhill Aerodrome in May 1985 and was probably damaged beyond repair

Percival Gull Six tuning its 200 hp Gipsy Six. **Below** Jean Batten's Percival Gull Six is currently under restoration and should by flying again in 1987. **Right** Percival P.40 Prentice trainer owned and flown by Bob Batt. During its RAF career the Prentice was usually flown as a two-seater, but civil versions were converted to carry up to six passengers

European exotica

Left Vivid Swiss Jungmeister HB-MKM. **Above** The
Bucker BU.133 Jungmeister must surely rank as one
of the greatest aerobatic airplanes of all time. This
machine served with the Swiss Air Force as a U-51
and then passed into private ownership as HB-MIM
before being registered in Britain as G-AXNI

Ex-*Flying* magazine staffer and now publisher of the British-based monthly *Pilot*, James Gilbert poses his very own Jungmeister, G-AYSJ. It is painted to represent the Jungmeisters operated by the *Deutscher Luftsport Verband*—the sport flying organization in pre-war Nazi Germany. According to Gilbert, 'It's the nicest aerobatic ship I've ever flown'

Inset The Stampe S.V.4 is probably the best product to come out of Belgium after Stella Artois lager. G-AWEF was converted by Rollason's to take the Gipsy Major Mk 10-1 engine and it is still active with the Tiger Club. **Left** Airline captains Brian Smith and Peter Jarvis become the 'Stampe Duo' on spare weekends. Their non-radio synchronized display includes this smoky 'mirror' manoeuvre. **Below**

Inverted Stampe S.V.4C flown by Iain Weston, one of the original members of the Rothmans Aerobatic Team. The photographer was looking aft, kneeling on the front seat of another Stampe with the harness strapped across the back of his calfs. **Overleaf** Danish Duo: KZ VII (nearest) and a KZ III designed by Kramme-Zeuthen and piloted by Jens Toft and Peter Thomsen respectively

In the quest for better aerobatic performance, Bob Mitchell acquired this 1949 KZ VIII, previously owned by the renowned Swiss aerobatic ace Arnold Wagner. Designed by Bjorn Andreasson, the airplane is of all wooden construction and it's stressed to a bullet-proof +/− 12 G. Using all the 145 horses in its Gipsy Major motor it is capable of three consecutive horizontal snap rolls. (Excuse me, I feel sick.) **Above**

Another firm aerobatic favourite is the Czech-built Zlin Z-526 Trener Master. It is powered by a super-smooth 160 hp Walter Minor 6. **Overleaf** Only a few examples of this 1954 Czechoslovakian L.40 Meta-Sokol tourer reached the West. Distinguished by its dainty reversed-tricycle landing gear, this all-metal four-seater cruises at 127 mph on its 110 hp Letadlovy